Introduction to Probability-Based Options Trading

John Andres

John Andres
john@optionsmeister.com
513.518.6666
Naples, Fl

Limits of Liability and Disclaimer of Warranty

The author and publisher shall not be liable for your misuse of this material. This book is strictly for informational and educational purposes.

Warning – Disclaimer

The purpose of this book is to educate and entertain. The author and/or publisher do not guarantee that anyone following these techniques, suggestions, tips, ideas, or strategies will become successful. The author and/or publisher shall have neither liability nor responsibility to anyone with respect to any loss or damage caused, or alleged to be caused, directly or indirectly, by the information contained in this book.

BUSINESS & ECONOMICS / E-Commerce/Online Trading
BUSINESS & ECONOMICS / Investments & Securities/Analysis & Trading Strategies

ISBN   978-1-7349743-0-0

Contents

Introduction

Hello, I'm John Andres from OptionsMeister.com and I want to sincerely thank you for purchasing my book, "**An Introduction to Probability-Based Options Trading**". My aim in this book is to acquaint you with a probability-based trading methodology and to show you how I use probability-based trading to generate consistent and profitable returns. I do not intend to force my thinking or the probability-based trading method on you, but merely to expose you to probability-based trading so you can make an educated decision for yourself.

I'm very consistent relative to what I say about other trading methods. In the many webinars and workshops in which I have conducted or took part, I will never condemn another trader's methodology. There are many, many ways to trade and believe me, I have tried most. I will explain to you why I'm such a strong proponent of this methodology and the advantages I have found to be so valuable for me and why probability-based trading has totally turned my trading and investing from mediocrity to consistency.

Probability-based trading has allowed me to be very mechanical, and unemotional. These are essential characteristics of a consistent, disciplined and profitable trader/investor. I encourage you to experience probability-based trading and find out for yourself how it puts the odds in your favor.

I will explain how to use the elements of probability-based trading and execute statistically profitable trades in 30 seconds with no technical analysis or fundamental analysis required. Put away your candlesticks, your moving averages, and any other indicator that you've relied on and sit back and enjoy the book. I hope that you will find probability-based trading as compelling as have I.

What I truly hope you will glean from this publication is that the method is not a one and done strategy. We base the very premise of this methodology upon odds and putting those odds in your favor. That means taking a lot of occurrences (trades) and allowing the math to generate predictable statistics. This book will present you with a trading methodology and all its criteria that I use every single day. I will not cover specific strategies in this book. My aim is as it states, an introduction to the method.

I want you to consider these hypotheticals:

1. What if you could predict your winning percentage for the entire year?
2. What if you could use a small fraction of your account, and achieve above market returns on your entire account?
3. What if you could define your risk at entry and have a 70% or greater probability of profit?
4. What if you can have an average of about 20 days in each trade?
5. What if you could make money when the market is not accommodating you? In other words, you don't have to be directionally right.
6. And finally, what if you could finally stop the insane search for the holy Grail, which we all know does not really exist?

The purpose for this book is to expose the reader to the probability-based trading method. And to provide the reader with enough information and clarity to understand the concepts and determine if probability-based trading is a fit.

The book will not cover specific strategies. I have authored a book titled "The 32 Most Common Option Strategies" that covers the metrics and mechanics of each strategy.

Use this book to build a solid option trading foundation and you too will be on your way to becoming the consistent trader you desire. Good Luck and Great Trading!

Chapter 1
Overview

I would like to welcome you to my book, "**An Introduction to Probability-Based Options Trading**". The intent of this book is to make you familiar with the concepts of the probability-based trading method. And how you can use the wonderful technology that's available to us today to predict your results and become a consistent, disciplined and most of all a profitable trader. Following the concepts of probability-based trading will further help you become a mechanical and non-emotional trader.

Foremost, the overriding purpose of this book is to expose you to probability-based trading. You may have never heard of probability-based trading. The information found in the book will present you with the advantages of this methodology. Also, you will see how to use the wealth of technology that we have today. And how to put that technology to use in determining trade entries. That will put the odds in your favor every single time you "pull the trigger".

Understand that this book will not be strategy specific. My aim in this course is to introduce you to the probability – based trading method. After grasping the concepts, I want you to have enough information to make an educated decision on whether this trading method makes sense to you. If like what you learn, then you can choose to use the criteria in your trading.

The goal for the reader of this book is to understand the basics of the probability-based trading method and how to implement it in his or her trading in a manner that is consistent and congruent with your trading goals. If you are fortunate enough to have a significant existing portfolio, I want to show you how to use probability-based training to enhance returns of that portfolio.

I enjoy working with clients on existing portfolios and show them how he/she must aggressively lower the cost basis of their long positions. Conversely, with short positions, raise the cost basis to increase the overall performance of their portfolio and not be subject to the market's normal ebb and flow.

If your goal is to generate consistent, predictable cash flow and maybe even replace your current income stream, I want to introduce you to a trading method that can help you realize your goals and aspirations. If you already have a enough monthly cash flow to meet your needs and your goal is to build wealth, I think you'll find that probability-based trading will help you achieve that most important goal.

Here is something to ponder:

> *"There are old traders and there are bold traders, but there are no old, bold traders"*

The reason is, being an old, bold trader almost assures "blown out" accounts. I've been there, done that so I can speak from experience. I want to show you how to trade the probability-based way, put the odds in your favor and mitigate your chance of blowing up your account.

As you start on this journey, I want to assure you that trading, specifically probability-based trading is a learned skill. Don't fret about whether you are smart enough to grasp the concept. Probability-based trading relies on pure math and statistics. Relax, you do not have to be a math savant. Everything you need to know is right in front of you on the option chain.

Chapter 2

About the Author

B efore we delve into the main part of the book, an "Introduction to Probability-Based Trading", I thought I would let you know just a little about me. Where I have been and where I am today at least relative to trading. This is not one of those big biographies about my past business interests, where I went to college and all that fluff. Just where my trading started and how it got to the point it is today.

I began trading stocks in 1990. We didn't have the technology, the internet access, and the internet speed that we are blessed with today. Some of you may even remember these old dial-up modems and how the phone answered the modem with those weird sounds.

It was crazy relative to today, but additionally there were not any direct access brokers. This resulted in much higher commissions, and the prospects of generating profits were a much more daunting task in those days.

But like most of the investors from that era, I relied on the information and the integrity from the full-service broker industry. I was too busy in my businesses and my related business interests to manage my own investments, or at least I thought so.

I trusted my broker to manage most my account. So much so I consented to allow my broker, Bear Stearns, to encourage me to manage my Roth Ira. It turned out to be a fatal mistake. With blinders on and the full faith that Bear Stearns would be fiduciarily responsible, I transferred my $250,000 Roth Ira them.

In less than two years. They left me with $13,000. Consider that this was a Roth Ira, so I had already paid the tax on it. To say it was financially and emotionally devastating to me was a huge understatement. It was at that point with my entire retirement account virtually wiped out; I vowed to never, ever let anyone touch or invest any of my money. If would lose my money, I would do it myself.

With that in mind, I got interested in training myself to becoming a self-directed investor. I attended my first trading class in 2003. That was in the heyday when gurus and courses were popular. Albeit many of those were scams.

I recall the first course I took was "Teach Me to Trade". It was one of those typical deals. You go to the hotel, listen to this seemingly great pitch and rush to the back room so you can sign up for the latest and greatest courses.

In retrospect, it merited the title, "teach me to lose money". This was in 2003, I was 54 years of age, with my retirement account wiped out. But it committed me to learning how to become a successful investor/trader. I spent many years and six figures in courses, seminars, gurus, indicators, black boxes, and anything else that I believed was the answer.

I added a trading futures contracts on the indices and options to my knowledge base in 2004. I must admit that those first several years were a challenge. I fell into the trap that the harder I worked, the better the trading results would be. I assumed this because in all my previous business endeavors and educational endeavors, that was the way it was. I soon discovered that nothing could be further from the truth in trading.

I spent an inordinate amount of time and money on anything I could get my hands on relative to trading. I assumed the more I did, the better it was. But after eight years of trying almost every style and method on the planet, I was still a card-carrying member of the 95% group that weren't successful.

One thing I knew for sure, it wasn't for lack of knowledge and commitment. So, I asked myself "what were the 5% doing that I wasn't doing"? Even with all this time and money spent on training and trading, I still couldn't figure it out.

This lack of consistency led me to probability-based trading in 2011. Like all the other things I had tried, I was full of doubt and concern. When I really committed myself to the fact that it relied strictly on probabilities and tangible statistics, the light went on!

The process started me thinking about probability-based trading and the relationship to options trading. Selling premium via options on stocks and ETF's seemed to make a ton of sense. I thought to myself, if 80% of the options expire worthless, then why in the heck do I want to buy options?

I began on the path trying to figure out how to be an effective seller of volatility and premium. I want you to know that I do actively trade every day. I also moderate in a live trade room where I provide trade real-time help. Additionally, I work privately teaching clients on how to trade putting the math and odds in their favor.

I finally have refined how I apply probability-based trading and I hope that I'm able to pass my knowledge to you and materially shorten your learning curve. I want to save you from the pitfalls I've experienced.

I want you to know that everything I do is in the public domain. There are no huge mysteries or giant math equations. No secret indicators or "black boxes." Finally, I want to assure you it really "Is Not That Complicated".

Chapter 3
Technical and Fundamental Analysis

Before we dive into probability-based trading methodology, I want to do a brief overview of traditional trading and the methods that most of us are familiar with in our past and current trading endeavors. I contend that most traders are directional by nature and the majority of traders are directionally long. Most traders aren't comfortable trading from the short side. That is in stark contrast to what typically happens in the financial markets. That is markets will melt down, but they rarely if ever would melt up.

It is fundamental analysis that most traders are very comfortable and familiar with. Fundamental analysis looks at samples of past financial metrics to see if the current values are high or low relative to the current stock price or valuation of the company. The assumption is that stock prices will respond in predictable ways based on those past metrics.

Technical analysis is reliant on charts and indicators. It counts the number of times that certain price behaviors have occurred in sample data in the past. The technician then assumes that the financial instruments will exhibit that behavior again. Familiar technical analysis indicators are moving averages, support and resistance areas along with hundreds of other often used tools. We've seen where the price will test those areas or not test them.

Trader's often combine a variety of technical indicators to find areas they believe the stock or ETF will react. All traders are familiar with "double tops", "double bottoms", and the like where the market should turn. Contrary to probability-based trading, I am not aware of any quantitative information depicting how often these areas work. The research that I have relied on has concluded that they work about 50% of the time. In my mind, that does not provide a tradeable edge.

Now let me expand a little on financial fundamental analysis. Fundamental analysis is the evaluation of the company's financial statements, the company's competitors, their market share and future expectations. Management personnel give guidance to the analyst to develop a forecast for the company results in subsequent accounting periods.

One of the most common metrics that we see all the time and most of us are familiar with is a price-earnings ratio. Many of the highly paid financial analysts base the preponderance of their analysis on this measure. Most analysts also evaluate the balance sheet. They analyze management decisions, company direction and try to extrapolate earnings.

With a calculated forecast of future revenue and earnings, the analyst estimates the future stock price based on a simple math. Then the price of the stock times the number of shares outstanding generates the total market capitalization. At this juncture it is at the discretion of the trader/investor as to whether the company is fairly valued, undervalued or overvalued.

If the value is high or low relative to where it the stock is trading an opinion is issued by the analyst. The analyst will then issue a buy, sell or hold opinion.

Probability based traders subscribe to the theory that markets are efficient and everything that is public information is already priced into the stock. And for that very reason, the probability-based trader finds absolutely no edge in using fundamental analysis to make trading decisions.Probing a little deeper, technical analysis is another way that "technicians" predict price targets. Where a stock may find support or resistance. They generate these areas on a chart by market activity such as past price and volume at those price levels.

Analysts do not measure a stock's intrinsic value. They have no concern about what the company makes, what the company does, the internals, or the future expectation. They pay no attention to company news. They use charts, candlesticks, other tools, and indicators we're all familiar with to identify patterns. Once they have identified those patterns, and resulting areas, they suggest the future price activity of the company.

Technical analysis counts the number of times certain price behaviors occurred in a sample of past data. From that technical analysis assumes that the price of the instrument will perform the same way in future periods at those different levels or exhibit that specific behavior. Technical analysts therefore believe that the historical performance of the stocks and markets are indications of future performance.

The probability-based trader subscribes to the random walk model where technical analysis is meaningless. Consider that each time the price of the underlying reaches either support or resistance or some other technical area, the odds are 50/50 whether that area will be breached. Therefore, when price retraces from a resistance level or bounces off a support level interpreted by a technical an-alyst, that is validation of the support resistance theory.

I have read compelling research that to my satisfaction proves that the market is random, and it absolutely has no memory. With that knowledge, I have learned to rely on probability and quantifiable results. The math never lies!

Chapter 4
Two Important Concepts

In the last chapter, I discussed fundamental and technical analysis. I provided an overview of what technical analysis and fundamental analysis are, or at least how they're perceived by most traders. In this chapter, I want to touch on two important points before we move on.

In the chapter three, I pointed it out that fundamental analysis relates to the value in the company based on the intrinsic value, the market forces, company news, corporate guidance, etc. Technical analysis equates to statistics. I will present you with a real-world analogy that will differentiate the two methods for you.

Imagine for a moment you're in a shopping mall. You want to invest in a high-profile store in the mall. As a trader using fundamental analysis, you would enter the store. Once inside, you would study the product assortment, store traffic, sales activity and a myriad of other observable metrics. You would seek out the store manager and ask for specific sales trends and information. Based on the information you have gathered coupled with a review of the public financial information, you would predict whether the future for this business is good.

As a technician, you would sit on a bench in the mall near the store and observe activity entering and exiting the store. You would totally disregard the intrinsic value of the products in the store. You couldn't care less about what products are in the store. Your decision about this company is all about the patterns or the activity of the customers. Is there ample store traffic entering empty handed and leaving with a lot of merchandise?

Contemplating this simple overview, that we have outlined on fundamental and technical analysis, you then probably want to ask yourself why statistics (technical) and fundamental analysis are so popular. The only conclusion I can come to is this, technical analysis and fundamental analysis are both easy to do and we had used them for decades.

The saying goes, "if we always do what we always did, we always get what we always got." I think this statement is very relevant to this discussion. Probability-based trading assumes that all price changes in highly efficient instruments are random. Everything there is to know about a stock or ETF is priced in. There are absolutely no secrets.

Here is an example to think about, and I know all traders/investors can identify with this example. The CEO of the company knows everything that's going on in the company. He knows what the future earnings will be. How many stores will open, how many stores will close, how many employees will be hired, terminated, etc. But when the quarterly earnings are released, the CEO has no clue how the market will react to these numbers.

I assume that every trader has experienced this. I know that I have several times. How many times have you owned a stock, they handily beat estimates and have glowing forecast of the future? The earnings are released, and the stock gets hammered? You think you've got a home run. The stock tanks and you shake your head in disbelief.

Conversely, how many times have you owned the stock and they come out with a disappointing report and disappointing future projections. The company conference call sounds like the world is ending. The big funds jump in buy the stock and the price spikes.

My whole point in this example is that everything that is public knowledge is priced into the stock. Consider, no one knows anything that someone else does. We think there is this secret stock group out there that knows something. The reality is we price everything that is known into the stock. If you accept that reality, you will understand and accept the premise of probability-based trading. You will discover that probability-based trading works in your favor every single day.

In conclusion, what really appealed to me with probability-based trading is the mathematical part. I am not an engineer, but I like math. I have always understood math and I like the fact that probability-based trading does not rely on looking at charts and graphs and moving averages.

Probability-based trading strictly relies on the probabilities right in front of us on the option chain. We can evaluate every single day because markets are dynamic. And dynamic markets move.

I use a methodology that is consistent every single day. One that made the most sense to me. There are very few variables that we deal with in probability-based trading. The simple metrics are the price, the implied volatility in the days to expiration in the cycle we are trading.

With the readily available metrics, we can always solve for the expected move. You will discover in a later chapter that 70% of the time price is contained within one standard deviation. This knowledge is the "edge" that allows the trader to make educated and consistent decisions regardless of market conditions.

Regardless of whether the market is historically high or low. Or the implied volatility is high or low. That the trader can make probability-based decisions on the correct strategy was very appealing to me. And with a statistically representative sample size, the math does not lie.

Chapter 5

The Math Never Lies!

In the previous lectures we've gone over an introduction of probability-based trading, but now I want to get into what really is probability-based trading. It's not some fancy set of indicators and "squiggly" lines. It's basically the application of mathematics, I call it applied mathematics. It's just like the known odds of flipping a coin or rolling a die.I think you agree that if you flip a coin; the odds are 50/50 the coin will come up either heads or tails. If you roll a die, the single odds are one in six that either a one through six will come up. If you flip a coin 5 times, absolutely you could get 5 straight heads or 5 straight tails, but if you increase your number of occurrences and you get up to a hundred or a thousand or 10,000 flips of that coin, the odds will be what the odd should be.

Similarly, if you roll a single die, there are 6 potential outcomes. Each outcome has the same percentage of occurring. A couple of rolls will not be conclusive but roll the die 1,000 times and you will approach equal distribution of each potential outcome. Roll the die 10,000 times and you will get ever closer to equal distribution.

That I could rely on the on mathematics and probabilities is really what appealed to me. I concluded, and I think you will too, the simple math provides quantifiable evidence upon which to make trading decisions.

I could do trades that are math based and are 100% quantifiable. I know if I follow the criteria and execute trades that meet these criteria, having completed enough occurrences or trades; the results are predictable.

Another way to consider the predictability to take it a step or two farther using the coin flipping knowledge analogy. If I flipped the coin, and it comes up heads I give you $2. If the coin comes up tails, you give me $1. Obviously, the odds are in your favor. You should encourage me to do this trade thousands of times. It is a sure-fire positive expectancy for you.

The coin flip example is obviously 50/50. But that is precisely what we do in probability-based trading. We use the criteria to put the odds in our favor, so that is our edge. Our edge isn't that the fact that the coin comes up heads or tails. Our edge is in having the proper criteria to put those odds in our favor.

Another element of probability-based trading is that we are only dealing with three known variables or metrics:

1. Price
2. Days to the expiration of the option
3. Implied volatility

With these known metrics we can always solve for the expected move of the financial instrument over a fixed period.

In a future chapter you will understand how to use the knowledge that statistically 68.2% of the time, the price of the stock will stay within the expected move range. This was the challenge that I encountered with technical analysis and fundamental analysis. I found that I just couldn't quantify fundamental analysis and technical analysis accurately like I'm able to do in probability-based trading. There's always remained some subjectivity when I relied on the other methods of analysis.

My experience with technical analysis and fundamental analysis is that it worked until it didn't. For example, a double bottom is thought to provide support. The reality is that the current price, when it reaches support, has a 50% chance of breaking support and a 50% chance of support holding. I cannot see a tradeable edge in that.

I have found trading with probabilities provides consistent, quantifiable results given a statistically significant sample size. This eliminates discretion. You can simply refer to the option chain or the probability of profit on spread trades, and you know precisely what the results are to expect.

Chapter 6

Another Important Concept

I n this lecture, I'd like to discuss important concepts of probability-based trading. First, I want to discuss the inherent dangers in using technical analysis. The biggest issue that I see in using statistics, better known as technical analysis, is the potential curve fitting. In other words, using technical analysis to yield a desired result.

I'm sure we've all experienced that before. My personal experience with using technical analysis over a long period is it works until it doesn't work? I have also experienced that technical analysis often generates "self-fulfilling" areas of support and resistance. I cannot produce quantitative data on the results that provides a tradeable edge.

I want you to contrast that with probabilities. They never change. Regardless of market conditions, given statistically significant sample size, probabilities always remain consistent.

For example, one standard deviation is always one standard deviation. We know that 68.2% of the time price will stay within one standard deviation. That is not 100% but given enough occurrences we can rely on this information for our trading edge.

Another important concept of probability-based trading is the "law of large numbers." This is the cornerstone of probability-based trading. The law of large numbers simply states that the larger the sample size becomes the closer the results will equal the expected mathematical results.

Previously I stated probability-based trading is the application of mathematics. As in the coin flip analogy, the same is true for any known probability. Another example would be of rolling a single dice. A die has six sides each with a different number and therefore each roll has six potential outcomes. If we roll that dice a thousand times, we expect the results to be each number appearing about 16% (1/6) of the time. That is the law of large numbers!

That is precisely what's so very important about probability-based trading. We put the odds in our favor and when we have a statistically significant number of trades; we have the confidence the results will meet the expected outcome.

Another key concept of probability-based trading is the random market theory. It's a cornerstone of probability-based trading. The essence of the random market theory is that tomorrow's results have no bearing on what occurred today.

Let me share with you some research which confirms the randomness of the markets. This research concluded the market has no memory.

They conducted a study of the S&P 500 for a period of over 60 years. The study comprised 15,000 trading days of data. The study recorded the close of the S&P 500 each trading day. This massive study counted the number of consecutive up days and the number of consecutive down days. The results confirmed that the financial markets had an upward bias while also confirming the randomness of the market. Regardless of the previous day, 53% of the time of the next trading day was up and 47% the next trading day was down.

If you further drill down into the information and the data, you will discover the number of consecutive up days and the number of consecutive down days were about the same. The study proved to me that the financial markets are random, and the previous day has no bearing on what the next trading day will bring. (Chart courtesy of the Tastytrade Financial Network)

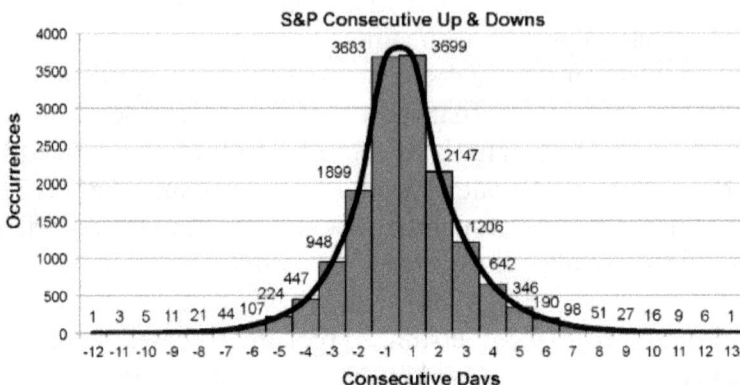

S&P Consecutive Up & Downs

You may ask yourself why then this methodology? First, it provided me with consistent, predictable results. The trader or investor can choose his or her winning percentage. I know of no other strategy that affords that edge. I can predict today what my winning percentage will be for the next year.

However, I don't know what the profitability will be. That all depends on the volatility of the market. If the volatility is up, the premiums I collect by being a premium volatility seller will be higher. If the market, it has a complacent year of lower volatility, the premiums will be lower, and the profit will be less. As a trader, it is an important to rely on a method that has a trusted, quantifiable winning percentage. That makes your job as a trader to find trades that meet your criteria, then execute the trade and manage the trade mechanically.

Another significant metric of probability-based trading is the trader knows implied volatility is overstated. Another study that covered the past twenty years showed in every year except 2008 actual volatility was less than the implied volatility.

Consider that knowledge for a minute or two. If you know the overwhelming odds are that implied volatility exceeds the actual volatility, doesn't it not make sense that you have a material edge as a volatility seller? You can sell options when volatility is expanded and likewise the price of the option is inflated. Then when volatility contracts, the value of the option decreases and you simply buy the option back for less than you sold it.

Another metric in the favor of the volatility seller is mean reversion. It is a known fact that volatility will revert to the mean. Price is not necessarily mean reverting, but volatility is mean reverting.

Think about the auction process for anything. Let's say we're in a grocery store, crowded with shoppers all looking for milk, but the store has only one gallon. That single gallon of milk will sell to the highest bidder during the auction process. Now assume as soon as they conclude the sale, a large truck pulls up with more than enough milk to meet the current demand. What would you expect to happen to the price?

The same thing occurs in the pricing of risk in just about everything. I live in southwest Florida. When a major hurricane is approaching, the insurance companies raise premiums to become congruent with their projected losses.

This is precisely the reason I want to use the probability-based method. I want to be the insurance company. I want to sell you a 30-day policy on the first of every month and watch it expire worthless, then sell you another policy next month. And simply stated that's what I do as a premium (volatility) seller.

Another "real world" analogy is the casino. The casino knows precisely what the odds are in every game that you play. The casino just needs to get enough patrons through the door and play the games, pull the lever or whatever, and the odds are in their favor. They have that statistical advantage.

And that's what we're attempting to do and are successful in doing with probability-based training. I know I have the odds in my favor and my job is to find enough underlying instruments, stocks or ETFs that meet my selection criteria. Then I just need to execute a statistically significant number of occurrences to make the probabilities and math work. I trust you see the comparison.

You might ask, if this probability-based trading method is so great, why don't most traders embrace probability-based trading? I think most traders and investors don't like to give up the "home run" stories. We love to go to the cocktail party and talk about the stock we bought it for "x" and it went to 10(x) or a 100(x) and I think that's that ego driven characteristic that we as humans possess.

That is not the case with being a premium seller. Using the probability-based trading methodology, the maximum amount of profit is the premium collected. That is just like the insurance company that collects the insurance premium from you. If you have an insurance claim, they cannot ask you for more premium post-accident. However, it would be reasonable to expect an increase in your next premium. In the casino's case, it limits them to the bet you placed prior to playing the game.

As a probability-based trader, you must embrace being a "singles" hitter. Just remember that the math works. If you follow the selection criteria in most of the strategies, you will have a 70% probability of profit. Do enough trades to make the odds benefit you. You will be consistent.

In a later chapter we will discuss managing the winning trades. We use a mechanical, non-emotional manner in which we make trade management decisions by 21 days to expiration. It is all about your embracing becoming a single hitter and not looking for those home runs.

There are many traders that don't give math time to work. They are always searching for the "Holy Grail". That search is not the answer. I call it the "bright shiny object" syndrome. You try a method for a short period, it works until it doesn't work. And then you are off to the next methodology, whatever that may be. They are doomed to a mediocre trading experience at best.

Remember, it is all about odds.

Chapter 7

Advantages of Probability-Based Trading

Now I will introduce you to the advantages of probability-based trading. First, there's no scanning for trades. One of the most frequently asked questions that I get is how do I scan for trades? To the shock and surprise from the questioner, I tell them I don't scan for trades at all.

Traders and investors, especially newbies, share a common belief relative to finding trade candidates. They believe they have to scan the universe of financial instruments to find that "needle in the haystack". They search every stock, option or future that exhibits some unusual characteristic that provides the trader/investor with a unique advantage. Most traders and investors seem to start with this premise. I must admit that I plead guilty to being one of them when I first started trading.

It took me several years of pursuing this path of trading to conclude that I was approaching it all wrong. The quest for the perfect investment of the day was fruitless and non-productive. There are over 7,000 stocks and ETF's. Add the thousands of options on those stocks, options on futures that have options available and you have nearly infinite choices.

The challenge to the investor that believes they can find the golden opportunity in this huge universe is daunting. The most important metric for trading the probability-based way is liquidity. I simply define that as millions of shares traded daily and tight bid/ask spreads.

I have accumulated a database of about 200 stocks and ETF's.

From this list there are 70 of those I trade most of the time. This list, pre-screened for the most important criteria, provides ample opportunities for the probability-based trader. So why waste time scanning for the needle in the haystack when in most market conditions you can find opportunities in this pre-vetted list?

Another huge advantage is you don't need to "grind" over trade selection. You are not wasting valuable time looking in every "nook and cranny" for that hidden gem. Find trades that meet the probability-based trading criteria and execute the trade. It's that simple!

As a probability-based trader, you need to put aside your compulsion to "be right". The reason is with probability-based trading most our trades are short premium. For short premium trades it is important that volatility has expanded beyond the mean. Some strategies do have a directional bias. But most of the trades the probability-based trader executes do not require he/she to be directionally correct.

The sole responsibility of the probability-based trader is to find and execute trades that meet the criteria. In most cases the trader should be able to find and execute a trade in 30 seconds or fewer.

A material advantage to the probability-based trader is the ability to pre-determine the winning percentage collectively for all the trades. As noted in a previous chapter, most of the trades I chose are in the 70% probability of profit range.

This is the foundation of probability – based trading. We can find and execute trades congruent with the winning percentage range in which we want to trade.

I select most of my trades that have a 70% area probability of profit (or POP). This POP coincides with the one standard deviation range. With the added edge of volatility expanded beyond the mean, the winning percentage is typically in the mid seventy percent range. I trust you agree that being able to predetermine your winning percentage is an advantage?

You might think to yourself, if I can pick my winning percentage, I want hundred percent winning trades. My response is if you want 100% winning trades invest your money in money market CD at the bank.

In this chapter I want to share with you my truisms for probability-based trading. First, foremost, and probably the one I emphasize the most is "**I know nothing**". When I say, "I know nothing," it always brings back memories of Sargent Shultz in the old Hogan's Heroes series. However, the reality is I know nothing! What I know is I do not have to know the direction of the underlying to be profitable with probability-based trading.

The fact is that no one has a clue how the market will react to any binary event. That includes the CEO and upper management company. Do not concern yourself with not knowing what will happen because no one knows what will happen. Find the stock or ETF that meets your criteria and execute the trades. Again, it's just that simple.

I previously pointed out that it is a known fact that implied volatility is overstated a high percentage of the time. This known fact is a very important metric we rely on in probability-based trading. Most recently, over the last 20 years, only in 2008 were there instances that actual volatility exceeded implied volatility. The preponderance of implied volatility exceeding actual (historical) volatility is a material edge for the premium seller.

It is also important to embrace that the financial markets are random. That the market has no memory. This is an important element in putting the odds in your favor.

It is a fact that overall the market has an upward bias. The upward bias is 53% compared to 47% of the time the markets display a downward bias. This just means that over a long period the market trends up. Do not let that dissuade you from also trading from the short side, or in the very least have a high percentage of neutral trades.

If you look at any chart of the past 100 years you can absolutely see the upward direction from the lower left corner to the upper right corner. Even with the slight upward bias, the trades you execute using known probabilities and the other key metrics will generate consistent, quantifiable results.

It is important to be keenly aware of some other probability-based trading truisms:

1. Understand that the financial markets are extremely efficient.

2. Also, everything thing that is known in the public domain is already priced into the financial instrument.

3. The law of large numbers. We need to have a statistically significant sample size, find trades that meet our criteria, execute those trades, and we will have a winning probability of profit.

Chapter 8

Keys to Success

I want to share with you the keys to success as they relate to probability-based trading. When I'm conducting webinars and seminars, I typically have a slide in the presentation that promises the best, most foolproof, indicator on the planet. As the attendees wait impatiently for the answer, I roll to the next slide in the presentation. To their surprise, there is a single slide with the word.... SIZE. Then I hear a large collective groan from the audience.

The truth is size kills. I've experienced that firsthand and I don't want that to happen to you. The devastating losses I took in October 2008 were strictly because I now thought I knew something. I was trading high probability credit spreads, and they worked great for 15 months. With such great success, I presumed I had a methodology that worked flawlessly. Month after month I saw my account grow. As I became more and more comfortable, I kept growing the number of trades. What could go wrong? I have been doing this successfully for over a year with zero drawdown. Enter October 2008. The sharp down move resulted in devastating losses. If I don't convey any other knowledge to you in this book, I want to encourage you to be very cognizant of your trade size and money management.

The first sign that trade size is too large to me is when a trader/ investor is uncomfortable after a trade has gone against them and panic sets in. When trading the probability-based trading methodology, you accept the risk at entry. Take a moment to process that.

Remember, we accept the risk at entry. Be comfortable with that risk and allow the probabilities to work for you.

We have discussed winning percentages and the other important trading metrics. Just follow the probability-based criteria and allow the math to work.

Ideally, we want to place short premium trades when the implied volatility is high relative to the stock or ETF we are trading. We use the metric, Implied Volatility Rank (IVR) to determine if implied volatility is expanded beyond the mean for the stock or ETF we are considering for a trade. IVR compares the current implied volatility of the stock or ETF to where the implied volatility of this stock or ETF has been over the last twelve months.

We use 45 days to expiration as our target for when to place trades. Obviously, 45 days to expiration only occurs once each option cycle. But we place trades throughout the option cycle until there are about 28 days left in the cycle. But 45 days to expiration is the "sweet spot."

This is precisely the essence of what probability-based traders do. They put the odds in their favor by using the criteria correctly and then execute enough trades to allow the math to work.

Once again, back to the coin flip analogy. The more occurrences (trades) that meet the criteria, the closer the results will be to expectations. You allow the odds to work as they should by keeping your trade size small and executing many trades. You're far better trading 10 trades of one lot each then one trade of a 10 lot.

It's Murphy's law. We always think we know what will happen. And with Murphy's law, obviously the opposite happens.

Another key to consistent probability-based trading is managing winners. I cover trade management in a later chapter. But for now, I want to share with you I typically manage winners between 25% to 50% of the premium received.

My typical target is 50% of the premium received. Example, if I'm doing a credit spread and I sell the credit spread and I collect a dollar in premium, I'm typically looking to buy that back for 50 cents. That will give you an idea of what I mean by managing your winners.

Managing winners is in strict contrast to what the "self-proclaimed" experts profess. Weren't we always taught to "manage losers and let the winners run?" Probability-based trading has proven this is not the way to consistency.

Trades are managed mechanically and non-emotionally when

there are 21 days left in the expiration cycle. At this benchmark we have 3 choices for trade management. Assuming the profit target is not reached by this benchmark, this is the mechanical management process:

1. Exit the trade for any profit or scratch
2. If the trade cannot be exited for any profit or scratched, roll the trade to a farther out expiration provided if the roll is for a credit or zero. We do not add capital to the trade.
3. If the trade cannot be managed according to either of the above steps, we remain in the trade. Remember, we accepted the risk at entry, and we let the trade play out for the remaining 21 days in the cycle.

Don't follow the advice from the "experts". They maintain "manage your losers, let the winners run." Probability-based trading proves this is not the roadmap to consistency.

Remember duration always trumps direction. We may have a directional bias when we trade, but we aren't directional traders.

It is worth repeating to quit obsessing with "being right." Allow our expertise and not our egos to drive our trading. Probability-based training is not about being right. Probability-based trading is finding opportunities that meet your criteria, executing those trades, and mechanically managing the trades.

I want to add just a few market facts to this chapter because they are key to success with probability-based trading. I have mentioned some in an earlier chapter; they are important enough that I want to reemphasize them:

1. You understand the markets have an upward bias. There is about a 53 to 47 upward bias.
2. Implied volatility is larger than actual volatility, the preponderance of the time. And that's how we make our living with probability-based trading. We sell premium when the volatility is beyond its mean. We are receiving more premium and expecting a reversion to the mean.
3. Implied volatility is usually mean reverting. As stated in point #2, we want to sell volatility when it has expanded. This is because we have every reason to believe it will revert

to the mean. It might not always revert to the mean in the cycle we're trading. But you can rest assured that volatility reverts to the mean.

These 3 facts are important to know and understand. They represent keys to success with probability-based trading.

Chapter 9
Standard Deviation

In this chapter I discuss standard deviation and how relates to probability-based trading method. Before you're freaked out by the term, or it brings back horrible memories of your statistics 101 class in college, please just sit back, relax. Take in how simple it really is and how we use it in probability-based trading.

I have shared that I trade the 70% probability of profit area. This is basically a one standard deviation range. We will delve into more detail with a graphic illustration of standard deviation using the normal distribution curve. A visual presentation will make a lot more sense to you. I place my short premium trades when implied volatility is expanded. Selling premium when volatility is high raises my winning percentage by a few points.

If math is not your strong suit, that is not a problem. Most option chains contain all the information you need. It is important for you to have a cursory understanding of what standard deviation represents. And you need to understand how standard deviation relates to selling premium, the probability-based way.

Drilling down a little further remember these simple metrics.

1. One standard deviation = 68.2% of the time price stays within this range
2. Two standard deviations = 95.4% of the time price stays within this range
3. Three standard deviations = 99.7% of the time price stays within this range

Most of the trades we put on are wrapped around the one standard deviation range. What does that mean? For example, we are selling short strangle on XYZ. It is trading at $36.00/share. The strike of the one standard deviation call is 41.00 and the strike of the one standard deviation put is 33.00. The price of the stock has a 68.2% chance of closing between 41.00 & 33.00 on expiration day. If price closes between the strikes, both options expire worthless and we keep the premium collected.

Conversely, there is a 31.8% chance that the stock will close outside the 41.00 to 33.00 range. It is as simple as that.

Another way to evaluate the trade is, the stock has a 16% chance of closing above 41.00 and a 16% chance of closing below 33.00. And 84% chance of closing above the short put and an 84% chance of closing below the short call.

On some trades we look at the two standard deviation range. This gives the trade about a 95% probability of staying within range. Three standard deviation moves are a black swan event and we rarely, if ever, place trades that far out as the premium for such a trade is too low.

Here is a graphic representation of standard deviation.

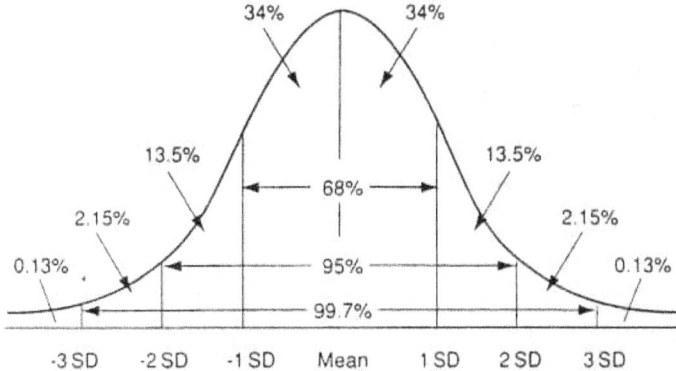

Undoubtedly you have experienced standard deviations in life experiences without even realizing it. Think of other ways in which you have seen normal distributions:

1. Grading on the curve in school
2. Health statistics
3. Life insurance and actuarial tables
4. Property and casualty insurance

With just about anything with a statistically significant sample size of data, we can develop the standard deviation ranges. And most of the time it will look like this log normal distribution we see in trading.

It is important to your trading that you to have an understanding standard deviation and its relationship to an underlying financial instrument expiring within or outside of its expected range. Over time, you find that most of our trades will wrap around one standard deviation range.

Referring to the chart above, and assuming that price falls at the center of the chart, we know that 68.2% of the time the price of that underlying will stay within that one standard deviation range. Just simple, basic math. I don't make this stuff up.

You will recall from the previous chapter that most trades entered at 45 days to expiration. We use the standard deviation range for 45 days. But you can use the standard deviation in any time frame you wish to trade.

Standard deviation is dynamic. That means it changes when any of the components in the calculation change. The most notable components are price of the stock, implied volatility and days to expiration.

Standard deviation gives the trader a known expected range. This knowledge is tradeable information. I want to emphasize this information, so you realize how significant this is. In the next chapter, I will illustrate how simple it is to find what you need to know on the option chain. And with that information, how to find and execute trades that meet the probability-based criteria.

Chapter 10

The Option Chain

In the last chapter, I provided you with a basic understanding of standard deviation. I want to reiterate that you can relax. It requires no math skills. Most option platforms provide the information right on the option chain.

You don't have to be a math savant to trade options the probability-based way. I trust you find it beneficial to have a basic understanding of standard deviation and how it relates to the probability-based trading method. And especially for short premium traders. Most of our trades are short premium, so we place trades where we expect the market not to go. Here is a screenshot of a typical option chain.

Open Int	Delta	Bid	Ask	Strike	Bid	Ask	Delta	Open Int
Mar 27, 2020 W			Calls	3d	Puts			IVx: 100.2% (±15.14)
745	0.96	42.00	42.40	200	0.50	0.52	-0.04	12.6K
286	0.94	37.10	37.85	205	0.75	0.77	-0.06	4.26K
1.25K	0.91	32.60	32.85	210	1.10	1.13	-0.09	9.63K
1.40K	0.88	28.00	28.30	215	1.59	1.61	-0.12	5.61K
4.70K	0.84	23.75	23.95	220	2.23	2.25	-0.16	4.69K
4.57K	0.78	19.55	19.80	225	3.05	3.10	-0.21	3.05K
6.41K	0.72	15.65	15.90	230	4.15	4.20	-0.28	3.31K
4.91K	0.64	12.15	12.05	235	5.55	5.65	-0.36	3.14K
7.77K	0.55	9.05	9.15	240	7.45	7.55	-0.45	3.59K
1.81K	0.51	7.70	7.80	242.5	8.60	8.70	-0.49	743
4.87K	0.46	6.50	6.60	245	9.90	10.00	-0.54	2.78K
1.26K	0.41	5.45	5.55	247.5	11.35	11.45	-0.58	1.19K
14.7K	0.36	4.55	4.60	250	12.95	13.05	-0.64	5.87K
1.64K	0.32	3.80	3.85	252.5	14.25	14.90	-0.68	710
3.19K	0.27	3.10	3.20	255	16.45	16.65	-0.73	1.63K
1.80K	0.24	2.58	2.61	257.5	18.15	18.65	-0.76	453
6.16K	0.20	2.13	2.15	260	20.45	20.70	-0.80	2.47K
1.86K	0.17	1.75	1.77	262.5	22.55	22.80	-0.83	363
3.13K	0.15	1.43	1.46	265	24.70	25.00	-0.85	702
1.26K	0.12	1.17	1.18	267.5	26.95	27.25	-0.88	914
6.59K	0.11	0.95	0.98	270	29.70	29.85	-0.90	1.62K
1.03K	0.09	0.78	0.81	272.5	31.55	31.85	-0.91	367
3.15K	0.07	0.64	0.66	275	33.90	34.65	-0.92	1.39K
1.41K	0.06	0.52	0.54	277.5	36.25	36.80	-0.94	719
4.41K	0.05	0.42	0.44	280	38.70	39.10	-0.95	1.35K
996	0.04	0.34	0.36	282.5	41.10	41.50	-0.96	297

- The puts are on the right side, and the calls are on the left side.
- The strikes are in the center column.
- The expiration date (Mar 27, 2020) is on the upper left.
- The one standard deviation strikes (16 delta) are 265 and 220. They are outlined in gold.
- The two standard deviation strikes (5 delta) are 280 and 200 outlined in green.

The outside column is "Open Interest" which indicates how many options are open at that strike on that expiration. I want to trade options that have a large open interest. Most platforms have a large variety of option theoreticals and greeks that can be interchanged in vertical columns to meet the trader's needs. You may be asking yourself, what does this have to do with standard deviation that we covered in the previous chapter and the probability of expiring out of the money? In this example the 265 call and the 220 put are the one standard deviation strikes. If you sold the 265 call and the 220 put that would be a one standard deviation strangle. That is the most common strategy that I choose to trade.

So how do those numbers equate to a one standard deviation strangle and the probabilities? The 265 call (at the time of this screenshot) has a delta of 15. You can add a column that gives you the percentage ITM (in the money) which is more precise, but I use the delta. There is a 15% probability of price closing at or above 265 at expiration.

On the put side the delta for the 220 put is 16. That tells us that price has a 16% probability of expiring below 220. Now to tie it all together: $100 - (15+16) = 69$. Therefore, in this example there is a 69% probability that price will close between 265 and 220 on expiration.

I do want to point out that there is a large equation that will give you a precise percentage number, but for our purposes using delta to select our strikes is fine. You can also consider the reciprocal. There is an 84% probability that price will expire above 220 on expiration day. $(100 - 16) = 84\%$. Conversely, there is a 85% probability that price will close below 265 at expiration.

I have also authored a book is specific on 32 different strategies. As I mentioned earlier, my favorite strategy is selling the one standard deviation strangle. The one standard deviation short strangle has a 68.2% chance of keeping the premium I collect. The odds are in my favor that the price of the stock (or ETF) will close between the two short options.

I also mentioned two standard deviations. I often sell the two standard deviation strangle for earnings trades and on large price stocks that typically are volatile. The importance of the two standard deviation strikes is that most brokers recognize those strikes as the maximum risk of the trade. It is a 95% probability that price will stay within that range.

The two standard deviation strangles are a little more advanced. I do choose to use them sometimes, and especially on large stocks and for earnings. As a new trader your focus for now should be on premium strategies wrapped around a 70% to 75% probability of profit.

Before concluding this chapter, I want to encourage you to embrace the math. What I mean by embracing the math is the probability-based trading method really appealed to me because it was something that was tangible and quantifiable. This math-based method was something that I could rely on whether the market was high, low, very volatile, or not so volatile.

The math is dynamic. The one standard deviation strikes may be closer or further away from price, depending on volatility. Another variable is the amount of premium you take in. With high volatility you will receive more premium at the same strike as in a lower volatility environment.

That you could have a consistent method that day in, day out, week in, week out, year in and year out that allowed the trader to put the odds in your favor and just focus on executing the trades is a "no brainer" for me.

This whole probability-based thing and the fact that I could hear something that's tangible and quantifiable just made an enormous amount of sense to me. I also accepted the fact that I had absolutely no clue of what the market or any stock or ETF I trade was going to do.

I have mentioned that before. You don't need to know the direction of the market to be a successful trader with probability-based trading. I've accepted the fact that the markets are random

I believe in the law of large numbers. I think that it makes perfect mathematical sense. The more occurrences we do, the closer we're going to get to the expected probabilities, Brownian motion, etc. Because the research is so compelling on all these areas.

If you've read any of Mark Douglas Books, I would specifically recommend you look at The Disciplined Trader because he states: you don't have to be right to know to be a successful trader. A just a wonderful book and one that is on top of my list in recommendations for any trader.

This platform in the screenshot is **Tastyworks,** which is my platform of choice. This is a very functional platform and the commission structure is very favorable for the retail trader/investor.

My referral link:
https://start.tastyworks.com/#/login?referralCode=TB44CWTAYF

As a special bonus to my readers, If you download and fund an account with Tastyworks using my referral link, I will offer a free one-hour consultation to get you started with the platform. Just contact me via email: john@optionsmeister.com or call me: 513.518.6666

Chapter 11

Probability Based
Trading Criteria

U p to this point in the course, I've laid out a fundamental basis for probability-based trading. I've reiterated how the tasks for probability-based trader is to find trades that meet his or her criteria than just simply execute trades. We can only put the odds in our favor if we have enough occurrences or trades that meet the probability based-trading criteria and then just let the math work.

Recall the coin flip and dice roll analogies? In this chapter I will share with you the criteria I use every day to find and execute trades. As you become more advanced, you will introduce some other metrics like option delta and beta weighting to your trading, but for now your focus must be on using the simple criteria in this chapter to find and execute trades. Let's get started!

First, we only want to trade **highly liquid instruments**. Those would include stocks, bonds, ETFs, etc. It is favorable if those instruments have an average daily volume of over a one or one million shares. Most of the underlying financial instruments I trade, and I'm happy to share that list with you, the volume is much higher.

We also want **tight bid/ask spreads**. This is very important. Most highly liquid underlying securities on our list will have tight bid/ask spreads. That means the difference between what the bid and what the ask is on the option chain are close to each other.

A tight bid/ask spread shows liquidity. When a stock has an upcoming binary event, an earnings announcement for example, even stocks that typically have tight bid/ask spreads may widen materially. And you want to avoid those instances. Bottom line, if you will enter a trade, you don't want to enter a trade and unless those bid-ask spreads are tight.

Implied volatility rank is really our secret sauce. We want to sell premium when that implied volatility rank (IVR) is over 30. I will cover examples later to explain how we pick that number.

Conversely, if you are looking to place a long (buy) premium trade, it is best to place those trades when the IVR is less than 25. I typically only look to place long premium trades when IVR is less than 20. The lower the better.

The other important metric is the **days to expiration**. My sweet spot is 45 days to expiration. Obviously, that benchmark only occurs once each cycle. I will place trades, in the current cycle, in the window from 45 down to 28 days to expiration. I am very mechanical and very disciplined about that. At the point I am below 28 days to expiration I am moving to the next options expiration cycle.

I avoid binary events in the expiration cycle I am placing trades. The exception is I like to trade the quarterly earnings releases with shorter expiration and often different strategies. I typically make 65 to 70 earnings trade each quarter.

As a condition for trades, I want a **high open interest**. A high open interest and high option volumes means there are a lot of players and a lot of contracts at those strike prices. When we are actively trading, we don't want strikes with low open interest. I refer to the trades with low open interest, "roach motels." You can get into those positions, but you just can't get out.

I also rarely, if ever, trade drugs and pharmaceuticals. Experience has taught me that most of the stocks in this sector will react radically to news. That news could be an FDA approval or denial. A case, or cases, where a drug has caused harm or just the opposite. When these types of news releases occur, the stocks are subject to severe spikes.

I will trade stocks like the huge conglomerates, Pfizer and Merck. These types of companies are so large and diversified they are not as materially impacted by a major drug release or negative news release.

I also choose not to trade biotech. Like drug and pharmaceuticals, they too are subject to a binary event that might occur every day with an FDA announcement. For all intents and purposes, I avoid these sectors.

Sector correlation is also very important to your financial future. I learned this the hard way. That is why I want to share this with you. I am now cognizant that I don't have too many trades in the same sector.

In the fourth quarter of 2014, I found myself very much over-weighted in oil and oil related stocks. That was a painful lesson and I want to help you from learning that same lesson. I now go to great efforts to make sure I am not over correlated in one sector.

Because it is so important, it bears repeating. Trade small size and trade many trades. It's the coin flip or dice analogy. The math works!

I always want to maintain risk discipline. What I mean by that is I trade horizontally, not vertically. Sound confusing? Let me explain.

In my early premium selling days, I learned the hard way. I have written many times in this book about the important of trade size. I cannot overstate the importance.

Trade size in the simplest terms is the number of contracts in each position. If you are a one lot trader, then you should trade one lot contracts in each of your positions.

As your account grows, and you can increase the number of contracts you trade, it is important to remain consistent with trade size. If you typically have 10 to 15 open positions or 30 to 50 open positions when you increase trade size go from one lot to two lots (or more) across your portfolio.

Don't suddenly think you know something and while most of your positions have a similar number of contracts, there is this one "sure thing" you go to ten lots or more on that one. And of course, that one goes against you!

Maintain that risk discipline! Keep it horizontal by trading about the same number of contracts in your various positions.

Relative to trade management, depending on strategy, I look to manage my winning trades at 25% to 50% profit level. For example, I enter a trade that generates $2.00 in credit per contract. My default exit is a $1.00 debit per contract. Hence, the profit is $1.00 per contract.

An exception to this rule is if the trade moves in my favor in a short amount of time. If I can exit a position for a 25% profit in 7 days or fewer, I will exit that position and redeploy the capital. My targets can vary slightly by strategy, but for all intents and purposes if you are a beginning trader and most of your trades are defined risk spreads, I would encourage you to mechanically manage your winning trades.

Chapter 12

Patience Grasshopper

I trust that by this point in the book you are getting your head around and understand the concepts of the probability-based trading methodology. I encourage you not to allow yourself to become frustrated. As the saying goes, this is a marathon, not a sprint. The financial markets will always be there. So, there is no rush. As you begin to find execute, and manage trades using the probability-based trading methodology, the criteria and the mechanics will become second nature to you. It may seem overwhelming initially but give yourself time to comprehend and internalize the basics.

Every trader learns at a different pace. Do not compare yourself to other traders. I would encourage you to begin "live cash" trading implementing defined risk spread trades in short order. I have witnessed many traders whom have excelled in "paper trading" only to fail miserably when they put their real cash on the line.

You are far better starting your trading journey with one dollar wide-spread trades. For example, you trade a one-dollar wide credit spread using the probability-based method. By properly following and executing the trade you are collecting $33.00 in premium. Your risk is only $67.00 on each one lot trade. Your probability of profit with strict use of the probability-based criteria is approximately 70%. You will not get rich in small trades like this, but as a newbie trader you will quickly understand the concept. Give it time.

Once you are confident that you are becoming proficient in the basic strategies it will be very easy for you to migrate to wider credit spreads. The mechanics are precisely the same. You still want to collect 1/3 of the width of the strikes and manage winners at 50% of premium received.

As a beginner, I would also add naked short (or cash secured) puts to your quiver of strategies. Naked puts are easy to manage and while they can go to zero, if you use the most liquid stocks and ETF's that probability is very low. From my experience and that of the many traders I've worked with, the biggest challenge I think you will face is executing trades that meet the probability-based trading method without being distracted by the vast amount of outside information that seems to engulf all of us. If you listen to the worthless financial commentary that is ever present, you will become distracted, confused and more than likely not consistent.

Suddenly you find yourself paralyzed in placing a simple credit spread on AAPL because some overpaid, self-appointed expert told you AAPL was going the other way. Remember, probability-based trading is not about being "right", rather it is finding, executing and managing trades using known probabilities. Don't forget, the math never lies!

It is worth repeating and I want you to internalize it. Probability based trading is not about being right!

Let me ask you a simple question. If you study 24 hours a day, seven days a week, are you going to change the results of the coin toss or the roll of the dice? If you flip the coin enough times; the results will be about 50% heads and 50% tails. With rolling the dice, after you have rolled the die a statistically significant number of time, each of the numbers, one through six, will come up about 16% of the time.

My point is, you could study until you're blue in the face. All that studying will have no impact on the results and that's the same math methodology in probability-based trading. You just need to develop the confidence in the mathematical approach. You must develop confidence and I think the only way to do that is to find, execute and manage trades according to what we have discussed throughout this book.

Now let me ask you a hypothetical question. You know you have the odds in your favor. You know the probability-based trading works. You know if you flip the coin enough times; the probabilities are 50/50. What are you going to do if you have six or eight losers in a row? Are you going to quit? Are you going to say this doesn't work and go home?

You need to realize that the math works and the more flips (trades) that you take, the closer and closer you will get to the expected results. I know that sometimes it is challenging to overcome, but you must overcome it. You got to put your faith in the math and know that the math does not lie.

I have discussed the importance of size and being too large in an earlier chapter, but it's so important to the success of the trader. The importance of maintaining consistent risk, and discipline allows the math to work.

There is a much more fatal reaction from trading large. That is the inability for traders deal with their emotions during a normal and expected drawdown. The trader acts emotionally and not mechanically.

Trust me, I speak from experience. I used to trade a hundred contracts each month on the indexes. I did great for about 15 months until October 2008. The emotional damage from that incident alone kept me out of the markets for almost a year. I don't want that to happen to you.

Remember, trade small size and trade many occurrences. You will be much better off. You will sleep at nights and be more successful. Trading two contracts each in 50 positions is far better than trading 100 contracts in one position. You could put the odds in your favor while spreading the risk.

Chapter 13
Proof of Concept

At this point you should have a fundamental understanding of the probability-based trading method. It is extremely important that you prove the probability-based trading concept to yourself. And that is not for a trade or two or even a month or two. I strongly recommend you do this for an extended period.

I have discovered the very best way to prove the probability-based trading concept to yourself and develop the confidence to just "take the trade" is to keep an accurate accounting of each trade. I know that you are no doubt cringing because none of us like to keep track of our trades and our results. We think we know what the results are, we can simply look at the gain or loss in our account. If you really want to develop confidence in the methodology, I found it imperative to keep accurate records, at least initially.

As the number of trades, you execute and manage accumulate, it will become apparent that you can trust the math. You will see with your own data the math doesn't lie.

I also want to point out how important it is to not react to each change in the profit and loss on the platform. That might shake your confidence. In fact, most trades that you put on are instantly negative because of the difference in the bid/ask spread. In most cases, your trades will be on several weeks. Give the time decay (theta) time to work in your favor. As a premium seller, theta decay is your best friend.

It is also important to realize how volatility affects the price of options. A spike in volatility (VIX) can have a material impact on the price of options and so to your platform profit and loss. The losses displayed on your platform are in most cases unrealized losses. Those unrealized losses can emotionally affect you if you allow them to do so.

Another issue with the P&L on most platforms is they can't keep track of rolls and other adjustments. The P&L could be very wrong in either direction, so it is best to ignore it.

In summary do not overreact of the platform P$L. Just continue finding trades, executing trades, and managing your winners.

I want to remind you to keep a record of your trades. You will find the way I track my trades makes a huge difference. When I initially started doing this, I cringed at the thought of keeping all these records. Now I continue to record every trade and it is almost a game. It only takes me about 10 or 15 seconds to enter a trade and 10 or 15 seconds to enter the exit.

I suggest you review your results periodically. It is not mandatory that you go to the lengths I do to trade detail, but it is a huge benefit to look back and see what is working and what is not. If you have results that contradict the probabilistic expectations, then drill down and see what you can change in your trading and strategy selection.

This worksheet details for me the number of each strategy that I have entered throughout the calendar year. It also tracks the current year to date profit(loss) on closed trades. This information is helpful in evaluating my trading and to make adjustments to my plan where necessary.

If you would like a blank copy of my Excel spreadsheet, I will be happy to share it with you.

Just email me: john@optionsmeister.com and request a copy.

As your proficiency increases in probability-based trading, you may get by with just monitoring your results on the platform. You will have accumulated enough knowledge to understand where your positions are relative to being profitable or not.

Chapter 14
Business or Hobby?

By now I trust you have gotten familiar with the probability-based method to the point you are finding, executing and managing conservative spread trades and perhaps some short naked puts. I hope you've been able to assimilate enough information to decide whether the probability-based trading methodology is congruent with your ideas of trading risk management and potential return goals.

As you begin your trading journey with the probability-based method or any other trading method, it is critical to assess your skill level. Remember, there's no hurry. The financial markets will always be here. Take your time and treat trading as a business and not a hobby.

There are many unsuccessful traders that I have known with an approach to trading that is haphazard and lacks the skill and discipline to be consistent. They treat trading like a game and not a business. They do not want to take the time and effort to immerse themselves in learning a method with a positive expectancy. And their results show it!

I can assure you, if you don't approach trading as a business, those that do, including the professional traders and the market makers, will take your money. That is the reason I recommend you honestly assess your skill level and I mean be honest. You are only lying to yourself if you attempt to trade beyond your skill level. If you follow the path I have laid out in this book and take the methodical steps, you will succeed. If you start by jumping in the "deep end" of the trading pool, expect the professionals to take advantage of you.

If you trade at a more advanced level than your current knowledge level, there are only two potential outcomes: 1. you might just be lucky in the short run, or 2. you will blow out your trading account.

If you are a total newbie, there are several trade basic strategies I have outlined in an earlier chapter with which you can start your trading path. I define those strategies as credit spread trades, debit spread trades and short naked puts.

I have a grouped 11 different strategies (including those mentioned) into "Trade Level One" strategies. These trade strategies are suitable for beginners. I would encourage you to add the others to your strategy quiver as soon as you have become proficient with the five basic spread trades.

Trade level one strategies start from the very basic and migrate to slightly more complex ones. As your skill level improves, you can do all those strategies found in trade level one.

As your trading skill continues to advance, you will move to intermediate level strategies. I define these strategies as Trade Level Two. These additional trade strategies are slightly more advanced. Some are undefined risk but should be very manageable for your skill level within six months, provided you have built that sound foundation from trade level one.

The final group, Trade Level 3 strategies, are the most advanced. Every strategy in this group is an undefined risk trade. However, I do not want that to discourage you from learning them. Because these strategies have unlimited risk, they require advanced skill in trade management. As your expertise increases, it will become clearer as what is the real risk in Trade Level 3 strategies. Armed with that knowledge, you will gain confidence in your ability to find, execute and manage these trade strategies.

As a trader/investor, it is important to ask yourself an important question. "Are you more concerned with your return percentage or the size of the winners?" It would not surprise me if nearly 100% of the respondents would tell me the size of the winners.

It is a "no-brainer" to realize that we all are seeking a return on our capital. But likewise we like to feed our egos. We want to go our friends cocktail party and say, "I bought stock XYZ for $10.00 and sold for 10 or 20 times that amount." As a probability-based trader your focus and ultimate results will come from small, consistent winning trades that yield a very good return of capital on an annualized basis.

Bottom line, you won't be the party goer bragging about your huge winner. You will generate consistently above market average returns, putting the odds in your favor with the probability-based method.

Consider the fact that most traders only understand and use the "buy and hold" strategy of investing. The risks with the buy and hold methods should be very apparent. You use a high percentage of your capital. That capital is always at risk. And you do nothing to improve the cost basis of your financial portfolio.

If you give your money to a money market manager or professional, naturally they will invest 100% of your capital. Those "self-proclaimed" professionals are, in most cases, compensated on your assets under management. Sure, they want to see gains in your account. That is self-serving. But the bottom line is they do not get paid on performance. We compensate them on how much of your hard-earned money they have under management.

It is a fact that most investors are only long. With a long portfolio, the owner of the portfolio can only have growth if the economy and the financial markets show year over year improvement. Consider that for a moment. You are paying a professional to manage your account that is solely reliant on the economy. Consider, if a calendar year has negative returns and your portfolio had a negative return, you still pay an advisement fee. Do you think that is fair?

Most investors are not comfortable having investments on the short side. Or they don't understand how to use investment vehicles that increase in a declining market or have a negative correlation to the stock indexes and the general market. As a trader/investor, it is important to understand how your portfolio is correlated to the S&P and other indices.

Another challenge with buy and hold investing is the returns, in most cases, are commensurate with the overall market. Over the last 100+ years, the S&P has averaged 5.91% annual return. Any buy and hold strategy must be directionally right. That is the advantage to probability-based trading. We don't have to be directionally right. We don't have to figure it out. And that is in stark contrast to buy and hold investing.

Most professional managers charge 1% to 2% of assets under

management. It is highly unlikely that a professional can generate returns equal to the overall market (S&P). After you pay the pro, it leaves you a return of 4%. As your trading proficiency improves, you will do far better, especially so after you pay him 4%.

A big advantage to probability-based trading is you risk less to make more. A probability-based trader never has 100% of his capital at risk. We typically risk from 25% to 60% of our available capital. The amount of risk capital varies on the current implied volatility as measured by the VIX. Contrary to what you might think, the higher the volatility, the more of our capital we want to deploy. Higher volatility means a higher premium collected, and we take advantage of that.

Chapter 15

What You
Need to Consider

Istated in the introduction that this book would not be strategy specific. Rather than discussing the execution and management of specific strategies, I want to give you an overview of how I use the probability-based method in my trading every single day.

I want to clarify that these strategies aren't specific to probability-based trading. If you have been trading options, I trust that many of these strategy names will be very familiar to you. The difference in the way probability-based trader uses these strategies differentiates the probability-based trader from other trading methods.

I want to emphasize I'm not a fan of all the crazy names that traders have come up with to identify and differentiate various strategies. I have expressed that the names can intimidate the new trader. Perhaps that is the intention of the whole professional trading industry? They make it sound confusing so you will shy away from becoming a self-directed investor. I hope for the sake of your financial future you will strive to take your financial future in your own hands.

Consider that every strategy is some combination basic calls and/or basic puts. The strategies are long or short or variations of basic credit and debit spreads. Please don't allow the crazy names to overwhelm you. Remember, this is a marathon and the financial markets will be there when you are ready.

I stated in the previous chapter that I break down the 32 option trading strategies, which I use most often into three categories: Trade Level One, Trade Level Two and Trade Level Three. I have categorized the three levels by difficulty and risk. I have authored a book titled, "32 Most Common Option Strategies" in which I go into detail on each strategy. The book is available on the website or by contacting me in the OptionsMeister Options Trading Facebook group.

In the appendix you will find the link to the OptionsMeister Strategy Cheat Sheet. As you can see, I have color coded the trade strategy levels using "Green" for Trade Level One, "Yellow for Trade Level Two" and "Red" for Trade Level Three.

All the Trade Level One Strategies are great for new traders. A newbie trader should feel comfortable in executing any of the twelve prior to improving his/her skills to migrate to the other 20 strategies. I want to assure you that even though the 12 Trade Level Strategies are the most basic and where every trader should start; they repre-sent the cornerstone of everything I do in probability-based trading.

Trade Level two strategies are exactly what they imply. Those 10 strategies are slightly more advanced and require more knowledge of trade management. As your comfort level in options trading continues to grow, you will add Trade Level Two strategies to your portfolio.

Trade level three strategies are for the more advanced traders. Each Trade Level Three is what I classify as undefined risk trades. Those are great strategies to add when you become more profi-cient in options trading. These strategies afford you more reward opportunity. And sometimes, when the trades are initially losing trades, you can manage them to break even or to a small profit.

I want to add that even though these trade strategies have an undefined risk, the real risk in the trade is at the two standard deviation strike for the highly liquid stocks and ETF's we trade. As an expert options trader, you need to evaluate the potential reward versus the probable risk in every trade that you enter. Trust me, your confidence will grow and you will trade strangles, straddles, ratio spreads, etc. in no time. Be patient and learn the execution and management of the trades and you will have a lifetime of trading enjoyment and success.

Chapter 16

An Introduction to Trading Earnings Releases

I n early chapters I introduced you to the various strategies that I trade in the course of my normal trading day. Prior to finishing this book, I want to share with you I am a very active trader of earnings announcements. They require public companies to announce earnings periodically. Every stock that I trade, announce their earnings quarterly. These earnings are for the most recently completed fiscal period. And typically, there usually is a conference call from the CEO and the CFO that serves to report on the company and answer questions from analysts.

You may ask yourself, "Why trade companies just prior to their earnings announcements." This is the most volatile and unpredictable time to trade a company. Well, I like to trade earnings releases for a variety of reasons. First, I like the fact they're very short term. I put them on near the end of the trading day and in most cases I take them off shortly after the opening the next morning. So for all intents and purposes, I'm only in the trade from a few minutes to an hour.

Quick in and quick out! I like to have trades on that can provide a reward in a matter of minutes as opposed to the normal 20 days that I average in each trade. Consider that I am a member of the baby boomer generation and I often joke that for baby boomers, instant gratification is too slow!

I also believe that it is important to get winners on the board. We all need winners! On some occasions there is a long lull between our winning trades as the markets become more complacent and fewer short premium opportunities are present.

Earnings trades typically will have a material increase in volatility prior to the release of the announcement. That offers the premium seller potential reward using the probability-based method. If you choose to trading earnings announcement releases, I would encourage you to trade smaller size than you typically execute with your normal expiration period.

I rarely trade earnings directionally. I sell expanded volatility and sell options where I have a statistical reason to project where the stock should not go. I understand that is contrary to most of the trading publications you can find in the public domain.

I always sell premium and I rely on the immediate volatility contraction. I liken it to watching a balloon expanding as it is being inflated until the balloon is full of air. As soon as it makes the earnings announcement public, it's like sticking a pin in the balloon. That's how quickly the volatility comes out of the security that I'm trading. That volatility contraction represents a significant profit opportunity.

I would also add that trading earnings announcements is something that newer traders should consider. I recommend you stick to defined risk earnings trades. Adding these trades to your plan will accelerate the learning curve.

It is important to keep in mind that earnings trades represent the same statistical opportunities that the normal 45 days to expirations trades. Because implied volatility is so elevated, we can typically receive higher premiums and or be further away from price than we are under normal conditions. And it's all about the volatility.

I will offer an in-depth online course on how to trade earnings announcements using the probability-based method. If you'd like to make earnings trades a very important part of your trading plan, I believe you will find the earnings trade online course very informative. If you are a Gold member of OptionsMeister or have joined the OptionsMeister Options Trading Group on Facebook, you will receive notification of the release.

Chapter 17
Putting It All Together

Prior to your completing this book, I want to share with you some important considerations. Foremost, you ought to think about why are you trading? That question may sound trite, but it's very important to know your why.

If you don't treat it as a business, it'll just be a hobby. It can be an intellectually stimulating, but it will still be a hobby. Now, having assumed that you are trading for any of the three reasons we talked about in chapter one, you must have a trading structure. Having a trading structure is not any different from a business plan that you would develop for any business structure.

A great thing about trading is you can choose many, methods that fit your lifestyle and financial goals. Understand that you do not have to sit at a desk eight hours a day to be a successful trader investor.

You will need to have a list of stocks and ETF's in a watch list you will trade on a regular basis. Also have a plan on what criteria you will use to add or remove symbols from your watch list.

Are you committed to a methodology or are you always going to chase the elusive holy grail of trading? If I can impart any wisdom to you, find a methodology that fits your personality and lifestyle, then make it yours. I speak from experience here. My mission is to save you time and some pain you might endure in your endless search for perfection.

Another important consideration in your trading structure is available resources. Be honest about the available resources, you can allocate to your trading business. I want to emphasize not to allocate resources to trading that will put any additional stress on you. Your available resources dictate the amount of risk you will take on each trade and your overall risk as a percentage of your trading capital.

A misallocation of resources can not only be financially devastating, but also emotionally devastating. Proper resource allocation will always leave you in a position to fight another day. Do not take it lightly.

Remember, probability-based trading is a slow and steady method. There are no home runs. It's all about hitting singles. You will trade small size and many trades.

Another consideration is capital commitment. If you commit capital to becoming a self-directed investor after you have honestly allocated your capital, it is important that you maintain that commitment. Trust your structure and know that over many, many trades, the probabilities will work. Don't let the market shake you out on the first drawdown you experience. Losing trades are a part of trading. As a trader, you just never know when a drawdown is coming.

Should you use the probability-based trading methodology, you know full well if you follow the plan, the math will work over a statistically significant sample size. If you don't make a firm psychological commitment of your capital to your trading business, it will be easy to just say this doesn't work and give up or look for that next bright shiny object(trading method).

It is important that you establish reasonable goals and expectations for your trading business. In a previous chapter we discussed how probability-based trading allows you to risk less and make more. As primarily a seller of option premium, our goal is to retain a certain percentage of the extrinsic value we accumulate. Research has shown that it is a reasonable goal to keep about 25% you the extrinsic value in your account.

I want to caution you not to have a goal of doubling or tripling your account every few months. We've all seen that movie, and it does not end well. Be Realistic with your return expectations.

Chapter 18
Conclusion

My intention for this book was to expose you to the advantages of using the probability-based trading method. It is important that you grasp the concept that when you have the odds in your favor, your job as a probability-based trader is to find and execute trades that meet the criteria. Never lose sight of the fact that the math does not lie!

I trust you understand the trading the probability-based method is all about hitting singles and not home runs. As a probability-based trader, you will experience a high probability of profit. The level of profit you realize is reliant on implied volatility and proper trade management. And that includes managing winning trades at the mechanical targets that are a significant metric of the method.

As you gain more experience and confidence, you will become comfortable with the tremendous upside available to you by executing trades that meet the criteria. I want you to be fully confident that trading is a learned skill. There are no special physical skills required, like hitting a major league fastball or dunking a basketball.

Remember, it's all about the odds. Become the insurance company or the Casino and take control of your financial future.

I will be launching several new online courses specific to options trading. Be on the lookout for the release dates.

Again, thank you and should you want to connect with me, here is my contact information:

Email: john@optionsmeister.com
Phone: 513.518.6666
Website: www.optionsmeister.com
Facebook: OptionsMeister Options Trading Group

Appendix

Recommended Reading

- Trading in The Zone – Mark Douglas
- The Disciplined Trader – Mark Douglas
- Option Volatility & Pricing – Sheldon Natenberg
- Options as A Strategic Investment – Lawrence G. McMillan
- The Options Playbook – Brian Overby
- When Genius Failed – Roger Lowenstein
- Trading for a Living – Dr. Alexander Elder
- Mind Over Markets – James Dalton
- Markets in Profile – James Dalton
- The Trading Game – Ryan Jones
- Trading for Financial Freedom – Van Tharp

Resources

- OptionsMeister Database:
  https://bit.ly/2WLB6JC
- OptionsMeister Strategy Cheat Sheet:
  https://bit.ly/3byj0i9
- Option Strategies – By risk:
  https://bit.ly/3avVsKI
- OptionsMeister – It's Not That Complicated:
  https://bit.ly/3dAay45
  (Slide Dec)

- Consecutive Up Days and Down Days:
  https://bit.ly/3bB4VAO
  (Research provided by Tastytrade)
- Getting Out of Your Comfort Zone:
  https://bit.ly/2QU3AwW
- Mark Douglas – Trading Thoughts & Beliefs:
  https://bit.ly/2xudqyS